sweet & simple
WOOL
APPLIQUÉ

15 Folk Art Projects to Stitch

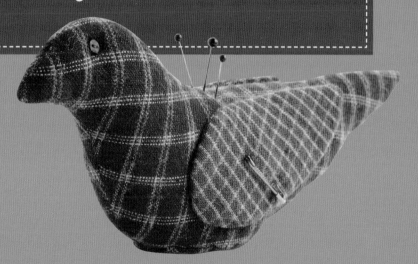

C&T PUBLISHING

Text, photography, and artwork copyright © 2017 by C&T Publishing, Inc.

PUBLISHER: Amy Marson

CREATIVE DIRECTOR: Gailen Runge

PROJECT EDITOR: Alice Mace Nakanishi

DEVELOPMENTAL EDITORS: Jenifer Dick, Edie McGinnis, Kimber Mitchell, and Deb Rowden

TECHNICAL EDITORS: Mary Atherton, Christina DeArmond, Kathe Dougherty, and Jane Miller

COVER/BOOK DESIGNER: April Mostek

PRODUCTION COORDINATORS: Joe Edge and Zinnia Heinzmann

PRODUCTION ASSISTANT: Jeanie German

ILLUSTRATORS: Lon Eric Craven and Eric Sears

PHOTOGRAPHY BY Aaron T. Leimkuehler and Natalie Turley

Published by C&T Publishing, Inc., P.O. Box 1456, Lafayette, CA 94549

Library of Congress Cataloging-in-Publication Data

Names: Nakanishi, Alice Mace, editor.

Title: Sweet & simple wool appliqué : 15 folk art projects to stitch.

Other titles: Sweet and simple wool appliqué

Description: Lafayette, CA : C&T Publishing, Inc., 2017.

Identifiers: LCCN 2017019289 | ISBN 9781617456176 (soft cover)

Subjects: LCSH: Appliqué--Patterns.

Classification: LCC TT779 .S98 2017 | DDC 746.44/5--dc23

LC record available at https://lccn.loc.gov/2017019289

Printed in China

10 9 8 7 6 5 4 3 2 1

birdsong in the
morning

CONTENTS

Appliqué Basics 6

by Renée Plains

Pinkeeps and Pincushions 10

 Bird on a Vine Pinkeep 12
by Renée Plains

 Cherry Tomato Pinkeep Necklace 16
by Lori Brechlin

 Honey Bee Pincushion 18
by Betty Edgell

 Little Sparrow Pinkeep 20
by Renée Plains

 Slipper and Large Strawberry Pinkeep 24
by Stacy Nash

 Wool Pear Pinkeep 26
by Marlene Strauser

Accessories 28

 Embroidered Heart Needle Book 30
by Anni Downs

 Flowered Heat Bag 36
by Anni Downs

 Land of the Free Jacket 40
by Debbie Duckworth

 Out on a Limb Notebook Cover 44
by Renée Plains

 Over the Nest Sewing Pocket 46
by Renée Plains

Page 12

Home Decor 50

Birdsong Pillow 52
by Anni Downs

Squash Blossom Table Runner 58
by Lori Brechlin

Quilts 60

A Big House and a Cherry Tree 62
by Renée Plains

Up on the Roof 66
by Renée Plains

About the Contributors 71

Page 66

Page 52

APPLIQUÉ BASICS

by Renée Plains

I love handwork because I find it so relaxing, and hand appliqué is one of my favorites. If you are new to this technique, here are some guidelines to help you get started as well as some other appliqué techniques used in this book's projects.

Needle-Turn Appliqué

1. Draw your design on the dull side of a piece of freezer paper (such as Quilter's Freezer Paper Sheets by C&T Publishing). Many quilt shops carry freezer paper. It's not just for grocery stores anymore!

2. Cut out the drawn design on freezer paper directly on the line.

3. Iron the shiny side of the freezer paper to the right side of the fabric being appliquéd. Be sure to leave at least a ¼˝ fabric beyond the edge of the design for a seam allowance to turn under.

4. With a pencil, trace the design onto the fabric. For dark fabrics, use a white chalk pencil. To prevent the fabric from slipping, place the fabric on top of a piece of sandpaper. You can easily make your own sandpaper board by gluing a piece of sandpaper on to a piece of Masonite.

5. Cut out the appliqué pieces, adding a ⅛˝ seam allowance. If the piece has curves, clip the inside corners. Fig. A

6. Place and pin the appliqué pieces on the background fabric.

7. Fold the seam allowance toward the back of the appliqué piece, tucking it under and creasing the design on the drawn line. Using a very small stitch, sew the appliqué piece to the background fabric. Start stitching from the wrong side of the fabric, coming up through the very edge in the fold of the appliqué. Then go back down through the background fabric right under the fold to create invisible appliqué stitches. Fig. B

------------ *Fig. A* ------------

------------ *Fig. B* ------------

Reverse Appliqué

This method works great for windows and other openings that are perceived to appear behind another appliquéd object.

1. Draw the necessary shape on the appliqué piece that lays on top of the background fabric and carefully cut a slit in the center of it. We used a rectangle for our example. Fig. C

2. Leaving a ⅛˝ seam allowance, cut out the center portion of the rectangle to reveal the background fabric behind it. Fig. D

3. Clip the seam allowance, particularly around curves and corners. Then tuck the seam allowance under and you're ready to stitch! Fig. E

Wool Appliqué

Appliquéing with wool is easy because you don't need to turn under the edges as you stitch. Here is a quick and easy appliqué method when working with this fun material.

1. Draw your design on freezer paper to make a template.

2. Cut out the templates directly on the drawn line, then iron them to the wool.

3. Cut out the wool appliqué pieces.

4. Pin or baste the wool appliqué pieces to the background fabric. It is also easy to hold them in place with tiny bits of Roxanne Glue-Baste-It.

5. Stitch the appliqué pieces in place. I use a primitive stitch (page 8), which resembles a buttonhole stitch (page 8)—only it is much faster.

-------- *Fig. C* --------

-------- *Fig. D* --------

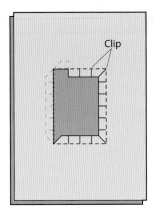

-------- *Fig. E* --------

Embroidery Stitch Guide

The projects in this book use a variety of hand stitches to achieve a folk art feel.
Here are the ones that you will need to know.

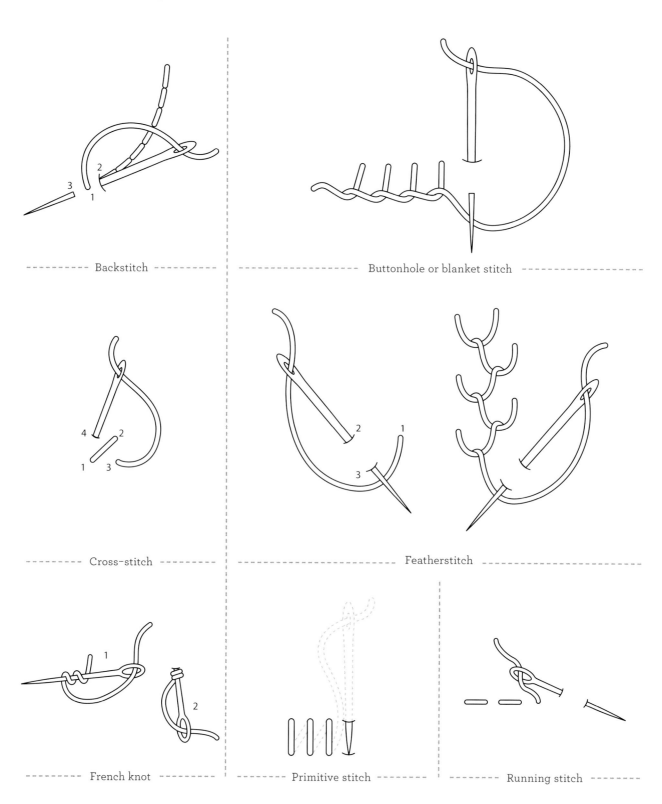

Backstitch

Buttonhole or blanket stitch

Cross-stitch

Featherstitch

French knot

Primitive stitch

Running stitch

----- Satin stitch -----

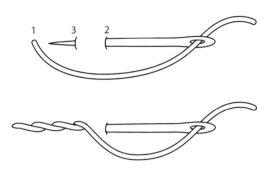

----- Stem stitch -----

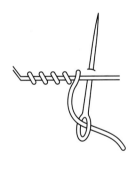

----- Whipstitch -----

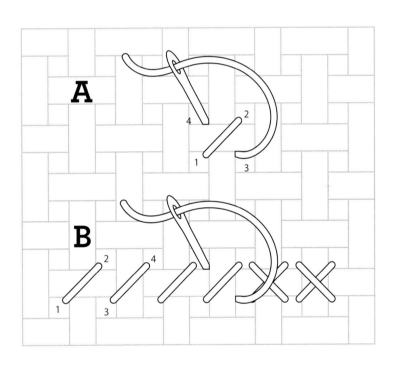

----- Counted cross-stitch -----

Method A completes each X as you go. **Method B** works a full row of half-stitches (/), then stitches back over the first half-stitches with a (\ ) to complete the X's. *Note:* It is important to cross all the top threads in the same direction (either all \ or all /). It doesn't matter which of those directions you opt for, but be consistent once you pick one or your stitches will have an uneven color.

Pinkeeps

AND

Pincushions

BIRD ON A VINE PINKEEP

Stitched by Renée Plains

I really enjoyed making this small pinkeep. The wool berries, leaves, and vines were especially fun to appliqué. I used toothpick-turn appliqué for the bird and wing. I learned this great appliqué method from my late friend, Laurene Sinema. It uses a round toothpick rather than a needle to turn under the seam allowance. Before you start appliquéing, moisten the toothpick by placing it between your lips. That bit of moisture gives the wooden toothpick a little extra roughness, which makes it easier to turn the fabric under as you stitch. Give it a try. I think you will like it!

MATERIALS

Fabrics

Linen: 1 fat quarter for pinkeep body

Cotton: Brown/black checks and brown print for bird and wing appliqué

Wool: Assorted greens and red for vine, leaves, and berries appliqué

Other materials

Small bead: 4 mm (approx.) for bird's eye

Small button: For scissor tab

Polyester fiberfill

Crushed walnut shells (Available at pet stores)

Embroidery floss: Dark brown

Cardboard: For interior base

CUTTING

Make templates from the Bird on a Vine Pinkeep patterns (pullout page P2) and cut pieces as indicated.

Linen

• Cut 1 rectangle 5˝ × 13˝.

• Cut 2 circles from circle pattern.

• Cut 1 piece from scissor tab pattern.

Cardboard

• Cut 1 circle slightly smaller than the circle pattern.

Cotton and wool

• Cut pieces from appliqué pattern (as directed in pattern).

Finished pinkeep: Approx. 4˝ × 4½˝

Sewing

1. Make a template from the Bird on a Vine Pinkeep pattern (pullout page P2) to use as a placement guide. Appliqué the pieces to the linen pinkeep body. I used a primitive stitch (page 8) on the wool pieces and needle-turn appliqué (page 6) for the bird and wings. Add the bead for the bird's eye.

TIP The small wool berries can be punched quickly with a Fiskars ¼˝ Circle Hand Punch. (My friend, Sue Spargo, shared this great technique with me.) Another easy way to cut small wool berries is to cut a ¼˝ strip from wool with a rotary cutter. From that strip, cut ¼˝ squares and then round the corners by trimming them with scissors.

2. With right sides together, sew the short ends of the 5˝ × 13˝ rectangle together to make a tube. Fig. A

3. Using a ¼˝ seam allowance, sew one of the linen circles to the bottom of the tube by hand or machine. It helps to pin these 2 pieces together at equal intervals around the circle in 4 places. Fig. B

Fig. A

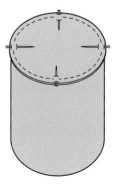

Fig. B

4. Turn the pinkeep right side out. Place the card-board circle inside the pinkeep bottom to help stabilize the pinkeep.

5. Sew a running stitch (page 8) around the pinkeep top ¼˝ from the top raw edge, leaving the ends long enough to tie.

6. Sew a running stitch around the remaining linen circle (pinkeep top) ¼˝ from the raw edge, leaving the ends long enough to tie. Fig. C

7. Fill the pinkeep with crushed walnut shells to approximately 1˝ from the top.

8. Gather the running stitch on both the pinkeep and the top slightly.

9. Fold the scissor tab in half lengthwise and sew with a ⅛˝ seam allowance. Turn it right side out. Fig. D

10. Cut a small slit for the buttonhole a scant ¼˝ from the finished end of the tab. Sew a buttonhole stitch (page 8) around the slit to finish the raw edge. Fig. E

11. Fold back the tab end about 1˝. Mark the center of the buttonhole on the tab behind the slit opening for the button placement. Sew the button in place. Fig. F

12. Add some polyester fiberfill over the crushed walnut shells, slightly rounding the top.

13. Place the linen top piece over the stuffing at the top of the pinkeep and pin in several places with the raw edges tucked toward the inside.

14. With the button facing up, tuck the scissor tab raw edge between the pinkeep top and side at a pleasing spot.

15. Sew a whipstitch (page 9) around the top edge, securely stitching the tab in place.

16. Using embroidery floss, sew a featherstitch (page 8) over the seamline around the top.

17. Add a small pair of scissors and button.

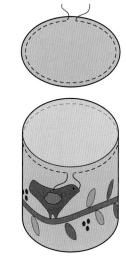

---------- *Fig. C* ----------

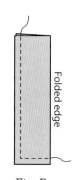

Folded edge

---------- *Fig. D* ----------

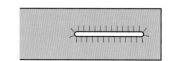

---------- *Fig. E* ----------

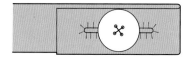

---------- *Fig. F* ----------

Stick a few pins and needles in your finished pinkeep, and it's ready to use!

CHERRY TOMATO PINKEEP NECKLACE

Designed and finished by Lori Brechlin

The summer months spent at Notforgotten Farm are peaceful and slow—waking to the sound of our beloved roosters and quietly sipping tea on our front porch is inspiration enough for my needle-work. The Cherry Tomato Pinkeep Necklace—a small token to wear while you stitch—is made from scraps of leftover fabric from your larger projects. It is a tiny reminder of gifts from the garden.

MATERIALS

Solid red cotton* fabric: 2 pieces 4″ × 4″ for tomato

Green wool: 1 piece 3″ × 3″ for leaves

Sawdust: For stuffing

Hemp cord**: 26″-long piece for necklace

Small white knitter's ring

Sewing needle

Cotton thread

Small, sharp scissors

Pins

White paper

Pencil

Chalk

* Or use wool, flannel, or another fabric.
** Or use heavy crochet thread.

Finished pinkeep: 2˝ × 1½˝ (not including cord)

Instructions

Use the Cherry Tomato Pinkeep Necklace patterns (pullout page P1) as instructed.

1. Place the 2 pieces of red fabric on your work surface, right sides together. Make a template by tracing the cherry tomato pattern onto white paper and cutting out on the line. Trace the outline of the template directly onto the wrong side of the top red fabric. Pin the fabric pieces together.

2. Using cotton thread, stitch completely around the entire circle by hand or machine. Trim away the excess fabric to within ¼˝ from the seam. Cut a small slit into the red fabric, being careful not to cut both pieces. Clip the edges and turn the project right side out.

3. Stuff the tomato firmly with sawdust, and then stitch the slit closed with cotton thread.

4. Make a template by tracing the leaves pattern onto white paper and cutting out on the line. Place the template on the green wool, trace around it with chalk, and cut out on the line.

5. Pin the green leaves piece on top of the stitched slit on the tomato, being careful to center it. Using cotton thread, make small whipstitches (page 9) to attach the leaves to the tomato.

6. Using cotton thread, attach the knitter's ring to the top of the tomato. Attach the hemp cord to the ring, and tie the ends together.

Now wear your cheery, little cherry tomato while you work to help mind those stray pins!

HONEY BEE PINCUSHION

Made by Betty Edgell

Bees, so necessary for pollination of fruits and vegetables, played a very important role in farm life. While most insects on the farm offered nothing helpful, the function of bees was quite the contrary. Bees play an important role in the pollination of blooms for fruits and vegetables, insuring a bountiful harvest. Besides a sweet treat for the table, honey provided another source of income.

FABRICS

Felted wool: Small amounts of gold, small plaid, and dark green

Flannel: 1 square 7″ × 7″ for backing

Embroidery floss: 1 gold skein

Crushed walnut shells: For stuffing (found at pet stores and some quilt shops)

CUTTING

Gold felted wool

- Cut 5 squares 1½″ × 1½″.

- Cut 4 bee bodies using Honey Bee Pincushion pattern A (pullout page P2).

- Cut 8 bee wings using Honey Bee Pincushion pattern B (pullout page P2).

Plaid felted wool

- Cut 4 squares 1½″ × 1½″.

Dark green felted wool

- Cut 2 rectangles 2″ × 3½″.

- Cut 2 rectangles 2″ × 6½″.

Finished pincushion: 6″ × 6″

Block Assembly

1. Using a generous ¼″ seam, sew a Nine-Patch block of 5 gold squares and 4 plaid squares. Press the seams open to reduce bulk. Fig. A

2. Add side rectangles and then top and bottom rectangles. Press to the rectangles. Fig. B

3. Following the assembly diagram for placement, appliqué the gold bee bodies and bee wings to the pieced block, using a whipstitch (page 9) with 1 or 2 strands of floss. Fig. C

Finishing

1. With right sides together, sew the wool top to the flannel back with a generous ¼″ seam all around, leaving a 2″ opening. Turn the project right side out.

2. Fill the pincushion with crushed walnut shells.

3. Stitch the opening closed.

-------------- *Fig. A* --------------

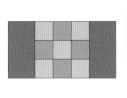 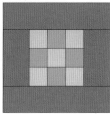

-------------- *Fig. B* --------------

-------------- *Fig. C* --------------

Assembly

LITTLE SPARROW PINKEEP

Stitched by Renée Plains

Like real feathered friends, these little bird pinkeeps delight the eye with their fanciful silhouettes and varied colorations. Use them to corral your pins or to create fun vignettes around the house.

NOTE *Give your Little Sparrow Pinkeeps different looks with other fabric combinations, such as a gold print body with gold print wings, red plaid body with red checked wings, or whatever variation you can imagine.*

MATERIALS

Tan check print: 1 piece 10˝ × 10˝ for bird body

Tan print: 1 piece 8˝ × 8˝ for bird wings

Cardboard: 1 piece 2˝ × 2˝

Buttons: 2 buttons, 4 mm size, for bird eyes

Polyester fiberfill

TIP To recreate the look of birds in nature, pick fabrics in similar hues for the bird and its wings. Because the wings are only partially stitched to the bird body, they create some definition while blending well with the rest of the piece.

CUTTING

Cut template pieces for the bird body, wings, bird base, and cardboard insert from the Little Sparrow Pinkeep patterns (pullout page P1). Cut the cardboard insert out slightly *smaller* than the drawn line.

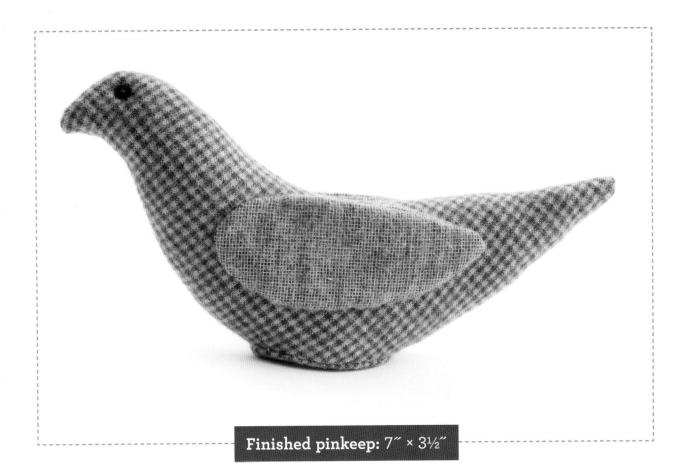

Finished pinkeep: 7″ × 3½″

Assembly

1. Bird body: Trace 1 bird body pattern on the *wrong* side of the tan check. *Do not* cut on the drawn line—this is the *sewing line*. With right sides together, place the piece of tan check fabric with the traced bird on top of the matching piece of tan check. Sew around the drawn line, leaving an opening as shown on the pattern. Trim a ⅛″ seam allowance outside the sewing line but leave a ¼″ seam allowance where the seam is left open. Fig. A

2. Bird wings: Trace 2 of the wing pattern on the *wrong* side of the tan print. With right sides together, layer the 2 wing pieces and sew completely around them on the drawn line. Cut a small slit through *1 layer only* of each wing. Turn each piece right side out through the slit. Then press. Fig. B

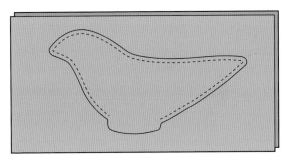

Fig. A

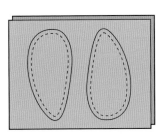

Fig. B

3. Bird base: Trace 1 oval bird base pattern on the *wrong* side of the tan check. With right sides together, layer the 2 oval pieces and sew completely around them on the drawn line. Trim a ⅛˝ seam allowance outside the sewing line. Fig. C

4. Stuff the bird firmly with polyester fiberfill. With a strong thread, sew a running stitch (page 8) around the bottom opening, leaving the ends long enough to gather. Gather slightly and tie in a knot.

5. Cut an X through *1 layer only* of the sewn oval bottom fabric piece. Fig. D

6. Turn the fabric oval right side out through the X slit. Fig. E

7. Slip the cardboard bird base insert inside the bottom through the slit. Fig. F

8. Place the fabric oval on the bottom opening of the bird with the slit side facing toward the bird to conceal the X slit. Whipstitch (page 9) the bottom piece in place. Fig. G

9. Bird wings: Whipstitch the wings to the bird body from point A to point B as shown on the wing template, being sure to place the slit side of the wing toward the bird to conceal it. Please note that part of the wing will *not* be sewn to the bird. Fig. H

10. Bird eyes: Sew on the buttons for the bird's eyes from side to side. Pull the thread slightly to create a little indentation.

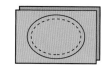

Fig. C

Fig. D

Fig. E

Fig. F

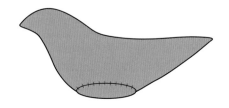

Fig. G

Whipstitch base.

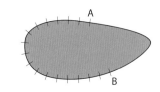

Fig. H

Whipstitch wings.

SLIPPER AND LARGE STRAWBERRY PINKEEP

by Stacy Nash

The little Slipper was typically made of silks, sometimes painted, and often had a little stitching and beadwork added. But I love this one, made simply in cottons. The Strawberry Pinkeep makes a darling addition.

MATERIALS

Slipper

Tan woven cotton:

1 square 7˝ × 7˝ for base

1 piece 3˝ × 5½˝ for top

Tan-checked homespun: 1 piece 3˝ × 5½˝

Thread: Needlepoint Inc. Silk Threads #911 Maple Brown Range (DMC 829)

Matboard: 1 square 6˝ × 6˝

Glue stick

Strawberry pinkeep

Brick red silk matka: 1 square 5½˝ × 5½˝ (prewashed)

Brown wool: 1 square 4˝ × 4˝

Thread:

Needlepoint Inc. Silk Threads #911 Maple Brown Range (DMC 829)

Ecru quilting thread

Sawdust: For stuffing

Assembly

Use the Slipper and Large Strawberry Pinkeep patterns (pullout page P2) as instructed.

SLIPPER

1. Trace 2 slipper base patterns on the reverse side of the tan cotton fabric. Add a ½˝ seam allowance as you cut around the drawn line.

2. Trace 1 slipper top on the reverse side of the tan-checked homespun and 1 slipper top on the reverse side of the tan woven cotton fabric. Add a ½˝ seam allowance as you cut around the drawn line.

3. Trace 1 slipper base on the matboard and cut on the drawn line.

4. Trace 1 slipper top on the matboard and cut on the drawn line.

5. Using the glue stick, apply glue to 1 side of the matboard slipper base and place 1 piece of the tan woven fabric base on top. Press to secure. Turn over and apply glue to the outside edges of the matboard. Fold the tan woven fabric around the edge and secure with glue. Now apply glue stick to the matboard pattern that is exposed and place

Finished pinkeep: 4″ long × 2″ wide
Finished slipper: 2¾″ wide × 5½″ long × 1½″ high

the second piece of the tan woven cotton fabric on top. Press to secure. Turn under the edges of the tan woven fabric and whipstitch (page 9) the 2 sides together using a strand of silk thread.

6. Apply glue stick to 1 side of the slipper top pattern and place the tan woven cotton fabric on top. Press to secure. Turn over and apply glue stick to the outside edges of the matboard. Fold the tan woven fabric around and secure in glue. Now apply glue stick to matboard pattern that is exposed and place the tan-checked fabric on top. Press to secure. Turn under the edges of the tan-checked fabric and whipstitch the 2 sides together.

7. Now attach the top of the slipper to the base. Place the top on the base with the tan woven fabric facing up. Use a strand of silk thread and start at the toe of the slipper. Whipstitch the top to the base just catching the cotton fabrics. *Don't stitch through the matboard.* Once you have whipstitched far enough around, you can pinch the top of the slipper so it arches over the base and continue stitching the pieces together.

8. Use 2 strands of silk thread to stitch the decorative straight stitch across the top of the slipper.

LARGE STRAWBERRY PINKEEP

1. Trace the strawberry base pattern on the silk matka and cut on the drawn line. Fold it in half, matching up the long edges and stitch, using a ¼″ seam allowance. Turn it right side out.

2. Knot the end of a 12″ piece of quilting thread and straight stitch around the top of the cone about ¼″ from the top. Leaving the thread and needle attached, stuff the cone with sawdust. Pull the thread to cinch the top closed and whipstitch to secure.

3. Trace the strawberry top pattern on brown wool and cut on the drawn line. Pin to the top of the berry base. Use 1 strand of silk thread to whipstitch in place and to stitch tiny X's down the seam. Use 2 strands of silk thread to stitch the seeds and to tie on the top of the strawberry in a bow.

WOOL PEAR PINKEEP

Made by Marlene Strauser

The Wool Pear Pinkeep is made from scraps of wool and stuffed with sawdust. Sawdust, straw, or horsehair was common material used for stuffing in the early 1800s, since they were easily accessible. This pinkeep could have been used as a toy or as a place to store pins and needles.

MATERIALS

Greenish-yellow wool: 1 piece 15˝ × 8˝

Brown wool: 1 piece 2˝ × 3½˝

Small stick: Approx. 2˝ long for stem

Ecru quilting thread

Sawdust: For stuffing

Assembly

Use the Wool Pear Pinkeep patterns (pullout page P2) as instructed.

1. Trace 3 pear body patterns onto the greenish-yellow wool and cut on the drawn line. Use a strand of quilting thread to sew the 3 pieces together, using a ¼˝ seam allowance. Leave an opening in one of the seams for turning.

2. Turn and stuff tightly with sawdust. Whipstitch (page 9) the opening closed.

3. Use a sharp pair of scissors to punch a small hole in the top of the pear, just large enough to insert the stick.

4. Trace 1 pear leaf pattern on the brown wool and cut on the drawn line. Place the leaf next to the stick stem and whipstitch in place using a strand of quilting thread. Wrap the thread around the stem a few times to secure.

Accessories

EMBROIDERED HEART NEEDLE BOOK

Designed and made by Anni Downs

I'm afraid my needle book collection is growing out of control, but I can't live without these great little organizers. The good thing about having such a large collection is that I can have one for every project I'm working on! This needle book has larger pockets that can easily accommodate embroidery thread, needle cards, and a multitude of other stitching supplies.

MATERIALS

Stitchery backgrounds

Cream print: 1 piece 7″ × 10″

Patchwork cover

Assorted colored prints: 9 scraps

Assorted cream/beige prints: 7 scraps

Lining

Cream print: 1 fat eighth

Inner pocket

Assorted blue prints: 4 pieces 2½″ × 3½″

Brown print: 1 piece 4″ × 8½″ for lining

Wool pin holder

Brown wool: 1 piece 3½″ × 5¼″

Blue wool: 1 piece 3½″ × 5¼″

Lightweight fusible fleece: ¼ yard

Embroidery floss: Stone #2326 by Weeks Dye Works

Button: 11 mm × 14 mm oval shell button

CUTTING

Cream print

- Cut 1 rectangle 4½″ × 6½″ for stitchery rectangle background.
- Cut the heart pattern (pullout page P3) for stitchery heart background.

NOTE *For both above pieces with stitchery designs, all stitchery should be completed before they are trimmed to their exact size.*

Assorted colored prints

- Cut 16 squares 1½″ × 1½″ for patchwork cover.

Assorted cream/beige prints

- Cut 16 squares 1½″ × 1½″ for patchwork cover.
- Cut 4 squares 2½″ × 2½″ for patchwork cover.

Assorted blue prints

- Cut 4 rectangles 2½″ × 3½″ for inner pocket.

Finished book: 4˝ × 6˝

Brown print

• Cut 1 rectangle 4˝ × 8½˝ for pocket lining.

Cream print lining

• Cut 1 rectangle 6½˝ × 12½˝.

Brown wool

• Cut 1 rectangle 3½˝ × 5¼˝ for inner wool pin holder.

Blue wool

• Cut 1 heart pattern (pullout page P3) for inner wool pin holder.

Fusible fleece

• Cut 1 piece 6½˝ × 12½˝.

Sewing

1. Referring to the stitchery guides (Figs. A & B) and to the stitchery photos (above and page 35), backstitch (page 8) the 2 designs, using 2 strands of embroidery floss.

Then trim the stitchery rectangle to 4½˝ × 6½˝ and the stitchery heart to size *after* the stitchery is complete.

2. Sew together a 1½˝ colored print square and a 1½˝ cream print square. Repeat for all 32 squares. Fig. C

--------- *Fig. A* ---------

Stitchery rectangle guide

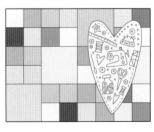

--------- *Fig. B* ---------

Stitchery heart guide

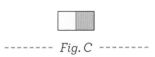

--------- *Fig. C* ---------

3. Sew 2 units created in Step 2 to make a total of 8 Four-Patch blocks. Fig. D

4. Sew together the Four-Patch blocks from Step 3 and the 2½˝ cream/beige print squares. The resulting unit should measure 6½˝ × 8½˝. Fig. E

5. Appliqué the stitchery heart from Step 1 to the pieced section from Step 4, positioning it centrally on the right-hand side of the block. Fig. F

6. Sew the stitchery rectangle from Step 1 to the left of the pieced section from Step 4. This completes the front cover. It should measure 6½˝ × 12½˝. Fig. G

7. Iron the fusible fleece to the wrong side of the front cover.

8. Sew together the 4 blue print 2½˝ × 3½˝ rectangles. The resulting unit should measure 3½˝ × 8½˝. Fig. H

9. Sew the 4˝ × 8½˝ brown print pocket lining fabric to the top of the unit created in Step 8. Fig. I

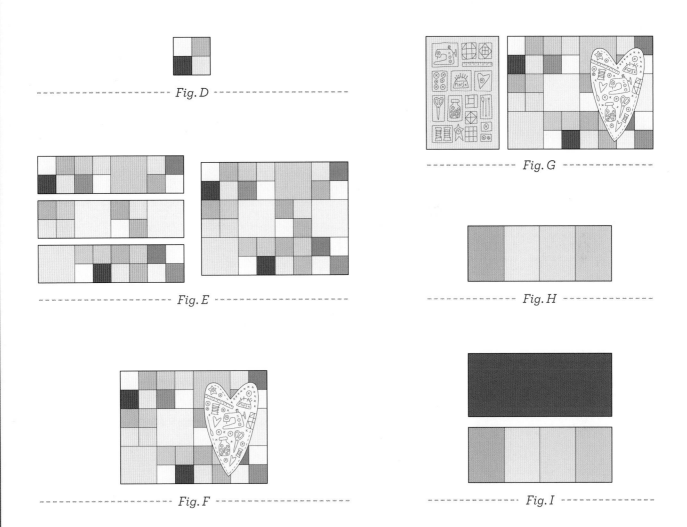

Fig. D

Fig. E

Fig. F

Fig. G

Fig. H

Fig. I

10. With right sides together, fold the unit from Step 9 in half and sew down the left side only. This creates the inner pocket. Fig. J

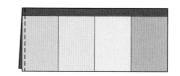

Fig. J

11. Turn the inner pocket right side out, then align its base and left side with the raw edges of the 6½˝ × 12½˝ cream print lining fabric. Baste the pocket in place. Using 2 strands of embroidery floss, sew a running stitch (page 8) along the pocket's center seam allowance and its right side to create 2 pockets. Fig. K

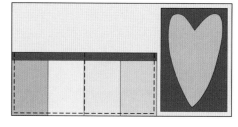

Fig. K

12. Referring to the Step 11 diagram for placement, appliqué the blue wool heart centrally on the 3½˝ × 5¼˝ brown wool background. Pin this piece to the right side of the lining fabric and whipstitch (page 9) it in place using 2 strands of the embroidery floss.

13. With right sides together, layer the backing cover on top of the front cover and sew around all sides, leaving a small opening for turning. Clip corners, turn right side out, and press. Fig. L

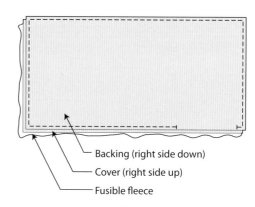

Backing (right side down)
Cover (right side up)
Fusible fleece

Fig. L

14. Using 3 strands of embroidery floss, make a button loop to the right of the rectangular stitchery panel. To make the loop, thread a loop through the fabric large enough to accommodate the button, plus a little more for good measure. Repeat this 2 more times to create a thick loop. With the same thread, use a blanket stitch and work around the loop, pulling it tight with each stitch. Fig. M

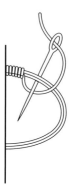

Fig. M

15. Attach the button to the right side of the needle book cover. Fig. N

Fill the pockets with all your needle packets, scissors, and thread skeins, and secure a few pins and needles to the woolen heart. Now you're ready to sew!

Fig. N

*This needle book makes a handy home for
needle packets and other sewing accessories.*

FLOWERED HEAT BAG

Designed and made by Anni Downs

This whimsical project combines gorgeous handkerchief linen that I happened upon one day and some wool that my husband hand-dyed. Together they make a calming heat bag, which works wonders for keeping your toes toasty warm or soothing weary shoulders after sewing all day. I even use one as a lap warmer on chilly days. To make the heat bag's cover easy to wash, I've included an inner bag filled with rice and fragrant lavender. You could also use wheat or barley as fillers.

MATERIALS

Appliqué background

Brown handkerchief linen: 1 fat quarter or ¼ yard

Appliqué flowers

Wool (5 colors): 1 piece 4˝ × 4˝ of each color
(I used gray/blue, caramel, beige, watermelon, and pea in various textures, such as herringbone and plaid.)

Patchwork section

Assorted cream prints: Scraps

Assorted colored prints: Scraps

Buttons: 3 light brown, 15 mm size

Inner bag

Cream homespun: ¼ yard

Long grain rice, wheat, or barley: 3–4 cups

Optional: Dried herbs such as lavender and essential oils for fragrance

Embroidery floss: Light gray/green
(I used DMC 646.)

Cream piping: ¼˝ wide, 1⅓ yards

> **TIP**
>
> **Piping:** I purchased ready-made piping for my project. If you can't find suitable ready-made piping, you can create your own custom version, using fine cording and fabric. Simply make a bias strip of fabric double the width of the cord, plus an extra ½˝ for the seam allowance. With wrong sides together, wrap the bias strip around the cord, and align the raw edges. Using a zipper foot on your sewing machine, baste the strip ⅛˝ from the cord. This stitched line will be hidden once the cord is attached to the heat bag.

Finished bag: 6″ × 15″

CUTTING

Brown handkerchief linen

- Cut 1 rectangle 6½″ × 15 ½″.
- Cut 1 rectangle 6½″ × 14″.
- Cut 1 rectangle 3½″ × 6½″.

Assorted cream and colored prints

- Cut 18 squares 1½″ × 1½″.

Cream homespun

- Cut 2 rectangles 6½″ × 15½″ for inner bag.

Assorted wool scraps

- Cut appliqué flowers, using Flowered Heat Bag pattern (pullout page P2).

Sewing

1. Referring to the guide (below), appliqué the wool flowers and leaves on the 6½″ × 14″ hand-kerchief linen background. *Before* appliquéing, note that 2¼″ of the left-hand side should be blank as this section will be overlapped with the patchwork section later. Using 3 strands of embroidery floss, backstitch (page 8) the stems.

Appliqué guide

2. With right sides together, sew together 2 cream homespun 6½″ × 15″ rectangles, leaving one short side open. Turn right side out, then fill two-thirds full with rice, wheat, or barley. If you wish, add lavender or other dried herbs for fragrance. Then sew the opening closed. This completes the inner bag. Fig. A

3. Sew 3 assorted colored and cream 1½″ squares together to create a row. Repeat 5 times to create a total of 6 rows. Join the 6 rows. The resulting unit should measure 3½″ × 6½″. Fig. B

4. Sew the 3½″ × 6½″ brown linen strip to one side of the unit created in Step 3. Press under. Set aside. Fig. C

5. Turn the left side of the 6½″ × 14″ appliquéd linen block under ½″. Then turn it under again to hide the raw edge. Topstitch this folded end in place. Fig. D

6. With right sides facing up, lay the patchwork section over the appliquéd linen block. Measure the width and overlap these 2 pieces so they total 15½″ in width. The overlap should be 1¼″. Then baste the top and bottom seams. This completes the heat bag front. Fig. E

7. Aligning the raw edges of the piping and the bag front, pin the piping around the entire perimeter of the heat bag front. Clip the seam allowance of the piping at each corner to help it lay flat. Using the zipper foot on your sewing machine, sew the piping to the heat bag front. Fig. F

8. Start and finish by turning the piping ends outward, away from the heat bag. Then cut off excess fabric. Fig. G

9. With right sides together, layer and pin together the heat bag front and back. Using a zipper foot on your sewing machine, sew around the perimeter. I finished off the seams with a zigzag stitch.

10. Turn the heat bag right side out. Referring to the project photo (page 37), sew the 3 buttons along the side of the patchwork section. Add hook-and-loop tape tabs to the underside of the patchwork flap, and secure. Then insert the inner bag into the heat bag cover.

You can heat this bag in the microwave for about 3 minutes, depending on your microwave's strength. To avoid overheating, test the microwave in 1-minute increments.

Sit back and enjoy the warmth!

Fig. A

Fig. E

Fig. B

Fig. F

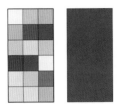

Fig. C

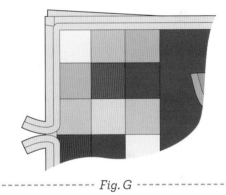

Fig. F

Fig. D

Fig. G

LAND OF THE FREE JACKET

Appliquéd by Debbie Duckworth

From December 1941 until August 1945, while servicemen and women were fighting, a dramatic change was going on in the homes and businesses of America. Our mothers, grandmothers, sisters, and aunts pulled together to serve for the greater good in their own hometowns. This project is inspired by these women and their needlework.

MATERIALS

Denim jacket

Embroidery floss or perle cotton: 7 colors—red, off-white, blue, brown, rust, gold, and black

Wool scraps: 7 colors

Red: 1 square 12″ × 12″

Brown: 1 square 12″ × 6″

Blue: 1 square 8″ × 8″

Off-white: 1 square 6″ × 6″

Orange: 1 square 6″ × 6″

Gold: 1 square 6″ × 6″

Black: 1 square 6″ × 6″

Needle: Chenille or embroidery

Embroidery hoop

Fine-tip permanent fabric marker

Tracing paper or tailor's chalk transfer paper

Scissors

Pins

Instructions

Photocopy the Land of the Free patterns (pullout page P3) onto copy paper and use as instructed.

WORDS

1. Center the words *Land of the Free* over the back of the jacket. (The letter "h" in the word *the* is approximately the center, leaving room for the star to be appliquéd at the end.) Center this over tracing paper or tailor's chalk transfer paper. Using a stylus or a pen, trace the words onto the denim jacket.

2. Using a stem stitch (page 9) or an outline stitch, sew the words with red embroidery floss or perle cotton.

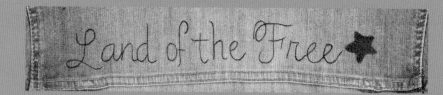

WOOL PIECES

Cut out the wool pieces, using the Land of the Free Jacket patterns (pullout page P3). Stitch the pieces down with a running stitch or a blanket stitch (page 8).

1. Large star   Add the blue star beside the words at the top. (See the detail photo, page 40.)

2. Crossed flags (Fig. A)   Stitch the pieces down in the following order:

a. Left flag and stripes

b. Right flag and stripes

c. Blue cantons

d. Brown poles

e. Black top of pole

f. Then stitch off-white French knots (page 8) onto the blue cantons to represent stars.

Fig. A

3. Back waistband garland (Fig. B)   Stitch the pieces down in the following order:

a. Brown vine

b. Blue leaves

c. Gold and orange leaves

d. Red flag

e. White stripes

f. Blue canton

g. Large gold flowers

h. Large red flowers

i. Small circle flowers

j. Then stitch the small vines using a stem or an outline stitch and the stars on the canton and the centers of the little flowers using French knots per the photo.

4. Collar flower (Fig. C)   Stitch the pieces down in the following order:

a. Blue leaf

b. Brown leaf

c. Orange leaf

d. Gold leaf

e. Small gold flowers

f. Small orange flower

g. Now stitch the small vine using a stem stitch or an outline stitch.

Enjoy your Land of the Free Jacket!

Fig. B

Fig. C

OUT ON A LIMB NOTEBOOK COVER

Stitched by Renée Plains

*I carry a covered composition book with me everywhere I go.
I especially love the ruled composition notebooks because they
come in handy when making lists or jotting down notes in my
fiber art and mixed-media classes. This project also makes
a fun journal for recording thoughts on everyday life.*

MATERIALS

Cover and lining

Brown/black check: ½ yard

Appliqué scraps

Assorted green wools: For leaves

Brown wool: For tree

Gray print fabric: For pot

Gray/blue dot fabric: For bird

Gray/blue plaid fabric: For bird wing

Binding

Brown tiny check: ⅛ yard

Other

Heavyweight interfacing: ⅓ yard
(808 Craft-Fuse by Pellon works well)

Button: 4 mm size for bird's eye

Black stripe fabric: Scrap for inside pocket
(*optional*)

Composition book: 7½˝ × 9¾˝

CUTTING

Cover

• Cut 1 rectangle from brown/black check.

• Cut 1 rectangle 10¼˝ × 15½˝ from heavyweight
  interfacing.

Lining

• Cut 2 rectangles 7½˝ × 10¼˝ from
  brown/black check.

• Cut 1 rectangle 4˝ × 10¼˝ from
  brown/black check for center lining.

Appliqué pieces

• Cut out the Out on a Limb Notebook Cover
  pattern (pullout page P3).

Optional inside pocket

• Cut 2 squares 5½˝ from black stripe.

Single binding

• Cut 2 strips 1¼˝ × width of fabric.

Assembly

1. Referring to the project photo for placement, appliqué the bird, leaves, tree, and pot to the front cover. I used hand appliqué for the bird, wing, and pot.

2. Sew on the button for the bird's eye.

3. Fuse or baste the interfacing to the wrong side of the cover.

4. To hem the 2 brown/black check 7½″ × 10¼″ lining pieces, turn the longer side under a ¼″, then another ¼″. Stitch the folded edge by hand or machine. Fig. A

5. With right sides together, sew a ¼″ seam allowance around the 5¼″ squares, leaving a 3″ opening for turning the pocket right side out. Turn right side out. Place the pocket on one of the lining pieces with the hem to the right side. Stitch around the sides and base of the pocket, leaving the top open for pens, pencils, and so on. Fig. B

6. Place the brown/black check cover right side down. Right side up, position the ¼″ center lining 4″ × 10 piece over the vertical center. Fig. C

7. Place the hemmed lining pieces right side up, aligning the raw edges.

8. Baste or pin the lining pieces. Bind the edges as you would a quilt.

9. Insert the composition book into the book cover.

Finished cover: 7½″ × 9¾″ (when closed)

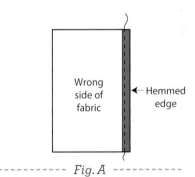

Wrong side of fabric

← Hemmed edge

Fig. A

Fig. B

Center lining piece 4″ × 10¼″

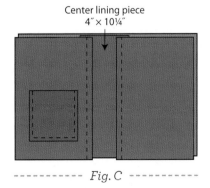

Fig. C

OVER THE NEST SEWING POCKET

Stitched by Renée Plains

Pack a small hand-stitching project with all your sewing supplies and you will always have a project to work on whether you're traveling or waiting for a doctor's appointment.

MATERIALS

Outer cover

Dark gray print: 1 fat quarter

Lining

Brown print: 1 fat quarter

Interior pockets

Brown/black prints: 2 fat eighths

Appliqué pieces

Wool scraps

Gold check: For bird

Dark gold plaid: For wing

Assorted green: For stem and leaves

Red wool: For berries

Notions

Button: 4 mm, for bird's eye

Binding

Gold print: ¼ yard

CUTTING

Outer cover

- Cut 1 rectangle 9½˝ × 18½˝ from dark gray print.

Lining

- Cut 1 rectangle 9½˝ × 18½˝ from brown print.

Interior pockets

- Cut 2 rectangles 5½˝ × 9½˝ from dark brown / black prints.

Appliqué pieces

- Cut out Over the Nest Sewing Pocket pattern (pullout page P2).

Double-fold bias binding

- Cut 1 strip 2¼˝ × 60˝.

> **NOTE** *It is important to make bias binding so the curved end of the sewing pocket will lie flat.*

Finished sewing pocket: 9″ × 18″ (when open)

Sewing

1. Referring to the open outer cover photo (below left) for placement, appliqué the pieces to the outer cover. Then sew on a 4 mm button for the bird's eye.

2. To hem each pocket, fold the long edge over a ¼˝, then another ¼˝. Fig. A

3. With right side up, align the first pocket with the bottom of the lining. Baste a ¼˝ from the bottom edge. Fig. B

4. Measure 1¼˝ from the top of the first pocket and draw a chalk line on that measurement. Fig. C

5. With right sides together, align the second pocket's raw edge with the chalk line. Then hem toward the bottom. Sew a ¼˝ seam from the raw edge. Fig. D

6. Fold the pocket back toward the top of the lining and baste it in place. Figs. E & F

7. With wrong sides together, layer the lining on top of the pieced outer cover. Round each of the outer corners by placing a quarter on each corner, marking the curve. Then trim the fabric from the corners. Baste or pin the 2 layers in place. Fig. G

8. Bind the raw edge, starting at the center bottom.

Open outer cover

Open interior

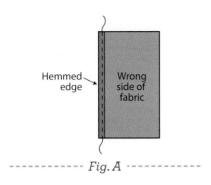

Hemmed edge

Wrong side of fabric

Fig. A

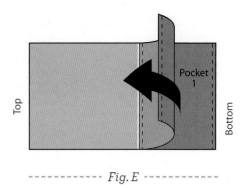

Top

Bottom

Pocket 1

Fig. E

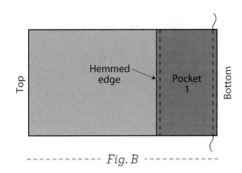

Top

Bottom

Hemmed edge

Pocket 1

Fig. B

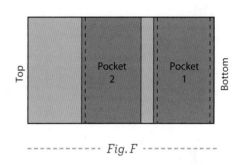

Top

Bottom

Pocket 2

Pocket 1

Fig. F

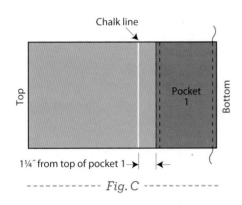

Chalk line

Top

Bottom

Pocket 1

1¼″ from top of pocket 1

Fig. C

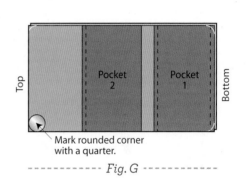

Top

Bottom

Pocket 2

Pocket 1

Mark rounded corner with a quarter.

Fig. G

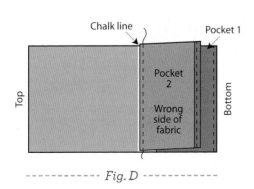

Chalk line

Pocket 1

Top

Bottom

Pocket 2

Wrong side of fabric

Fig. D

Home Decor

BIRDSONG PILLOW

Designed and made by Anni Downs

When it comes to creating an inviting home, pillows are a must. They represent hospitality, warmth, and comfort. A whimsical bird enlightens my patchwork pillow, while an array of wool blooms adds pizzazz.

MATERIALS

Appliqué block

Cream print: 1 square 9˝ × 9˝

Blue print: 2 scraps for bird and wing (I used a different one for each.)

Dark brown wool: 1 square ¼˝ × ¼˝ for bird eye (Bird eye center yardage listed in flower yardage.)

Brown print: Scrap for bird beak

Flowers

Beige wool: 1 square 8˝ × 8˝ (This is also used for the bird eye center.)

Dusky pink wool: 1 square 2½˝ × 2½˝

Pillow patchwork

Assorted colored prints (12): Scraps of each

Assorted cream prints: 8 squares 10˝ × 10˝

Inner border

Brown print: 1 fat eighth or ⅛ yard

Pillow back and lining

Cream print: ¾ yard (I used a cross-stitch design print.)

Lightweight fusible fleece: 1 yard

Embroidery floss: Light brown, brown, and dark gray / brown (I used DMC Khaki Brown #167, Hazel Nut Brown #869, and Brown Gray #3021.)

Beige rickrack: Jumbo width, 2¼ yards

Buttons: 3 buttons 1˝ wide

Snap fasteners: 3 fasteners (Or you can use 3 circular hook-and-loop tape closures.)

Pillow form: 18˝ × 18˝

Template plastic

CUTTING

Use the Birdsong Pillow patterns (pullout page P2) as instructed.

Cream print

- Cut 1 square 6½˝ × 6½˝ for appliqué background.

> **NOTE** *This block contains appliqué and should be trimmed to size after the appliqué is completed.*

Blue prints

- Cut 1 from bird body pattern.
- Cut 1 from bird wing pattern.

Brown print

- Cut 1 from bird beak pattern.

Beige wool

- Cut 7 from flower petal pattern.
- Cut 1 from bird eye center pattern.

Dusky pink wool

- Cut 7 from flower center pattern.

Finished pillow: 17˝ × 17˝

Dark brown wool

- Cut 1 from bird eye pattern.

Assorted colored prints

- Cut 43 squares 1½˝ × 1½˝ for pillow patchwork.

- Cut 3 from button tab pattern. (The tabs are cut *after* they're sewn.)

Assorted cream/beige prints

- Cut 31 squares 1½˝ × 1½˝ and 64 squares 2½˝ × 2½˝ for pillow patchwork.

Brown print

- Cut 2 strips 1˝ × 12½˝ and 2 strips 1˝ × 13½˝ for inner border.

Cream print

- Cut 1 rectangle 17½˝ × 19˝ for pillow back.

- Cut 1 rectangle 6½˝ × 17½˝ for pillow lining.

Fusible fleece

- Cut 1 square 17½˝ × 17½˝.

- Cut 1 rectangle 14˝ × 17½˝.

- Cut 1 rectangle 6½˝ × 17½˝.

Template plastic

- Cut 1 from button tab pattern.

Sewing

1. Referring to the appliqué placement guide (Fig. A), appliqué the bird to the cream print background. Please note that you will need to add a ¼″ seam allowance to the bird pattern if doing needle-turn appliqué (page 6). Do not add any seam allowance to the flowers. For the bird eye and center, place the cream wool bird eye center over the brown wool eye and secure it with a whipstitch (page 9). Using 4 strands of dark gray / brown floss (DMC 3021), finish the eye with a French knot (page 8).

2. Backstitch (page 8) the wording with 2 strands of brown floss (DMC 869) and the bird legs with 2 strands of light brown floss (DMC 167).

3. Set 23 cream/beige 1½″ squares and 23 colored 1½″ squares aside for the outer border and back of the pillow. Sew together 6 assorted colored 1½″ squares and cream/beige squares. Repeat once to create a total of 2 rows. Then sew these 2 rows to the top and bottom of the appliqué block. Fig. B

4. Referring to Fig. B, sew together 8 assorted colored 1½″ squares and cream/beige squares. Repeat once to create a total of 2 rows. Then sew these rows to the sides of the appliqué block from Step 3.

5. Sew together 4 cream/beige 2½″ squares. Repeat once to create a total of 2 rows. Then sew these rows to the top and bottom of the unit created in Step 4. Fig. C

6. Referring to Fig. C, sew together 6 cream/beige 2½″ squares. Repeat once to create a total of 2 rows. Then sew these rows to both sides of the unit created in Step 5.

7. Sew 2 brown print 1″ × 12½″ border strips to the top and bottom of the unit created in Step 6. Then sew 2 brown print 1″ × 13½″ border strips to the sides of that unit. Fig. D

Fig. A

Appliqué placement guide

Fig. B

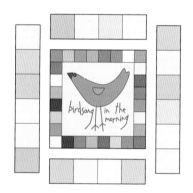

Fig. C

Fig. D

8. Sew together a 1½″ colored print square and a 1½″ cream print square. Repeat to create a total of 23 two-patch units. Eight are for the front and 15 are for the back. Fig. E

9. Sew together 6 cream print 2½″ squares. Sew a two-patch unit from Step 8 to one end of the strip of cream print squares. Repeat once to create a total of 2 rows. Then sew them to the top and bottom of the unit created in Step 8. Fig. F

10. Referring to the Fig. F top left and bottom right units, sew 6 two-patch units into sets of 3 to create a total of 2 six-patch units.

11. Sew together 7 cream print 2½″ squares. Referring to Fig. F, sew a six-patch unit to one end of the cream print square strip. Repeat once to create a total of 2 rows. Then sew them to the sides of the unit created in Step 9.

12. Referring to Wool Appliqué (page 7) and the project photo (page 53) for appliqué placement, appliqué the beige wool flowers and dusky pink wool flower centers on the pillow front.

13. Iron the 17½″ square fusible fleece to the wrong side of the pillow front.

14. To determine the amount of rickrack you will need, place the rickrack along the pillow top. Before cutting the rickrack, make sure its "mountains" are placed evenly along each length. Then trim the edge of the rickrack so the valley measures a generous ¼″. Fig. G

15. Pin the rickrack along each edge of the pillow front and baste in place. Fig. H

---------------- Fig. E ----------------

---------------- Fig. F ----------------

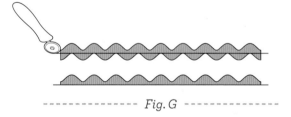

---------------- Fig. G ----------------

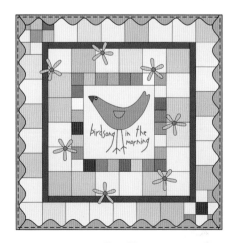

---------------- Fig. H ----------------

16. Using the remaining 15 two-patch units, make a total of 6 four-patch units. You will have 3 two-patch units left over. Fig. I

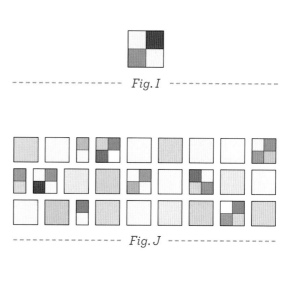

Fig. I

17. Sew together the 18 cream print 2½˝ squares, 6 four-patch units, and 3 two-patch units into 3 rows. The more randomly the blocks are placed, the better they will look. Fig. J

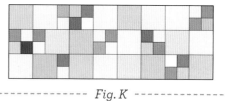

Fig. J

18. Join the 3 rows from Step 17. The resulting section should measure 6½˝ × 17½˝. Fig. K

19. Iron the 6½˝ × 17½˝ fusible fleece to the back of the section created in Step 18.

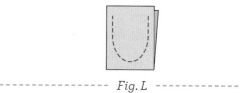

Fig. K

20. For the button tab, fold the blue print scrap in half with right sides together. Using a wash-out pencil, trace the template on the blue print scrap. Using a small machine stitch, sew on the drawn line, leaving the straight edge open. Leaving about an ⅛˝ seam allowance, cut out the button tab. Turn right side out and press. Repeat twice to make a total of 3 button tabs. Fig. L

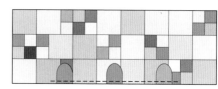

Fig. L

21. Centering the button tabs 2¾˝ apart, baste them to the base of the 6½˝ × 17½˝ pieced pillow back. Fig. M

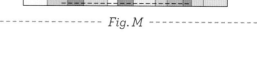

Fig. M

22. With right sides together, sew the base of the 6½˝ × 17½˝ pillow back lining to the base of the 6½˝ × 17½˝ pieced pillow back, sandwiching the tabs in between. Then turn right side up and press. Fig. N

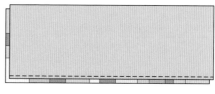

Fig. N

23. Iron the 14˝ × 17½˝ fusible fleece piece to the wrong side of the 17½˝ × 19˝ cream print pillow back piece, aligning the base and side seams. Then fold the top back down 2½˝. Fold it over another 2½˝ to disguise the raw edge. Then topstitch the folded edge in place. Fig. O

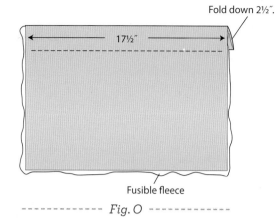

Fold down 2½˝.

17½˝

Fusible fleece

Fig. O

24. Lay the pieced pillow back over the cream print pillow back portion so the right sides face up. Measure the height and overlap the pieces so they measure 17½˝ from top to bottom. The overlap should be 2¾˝. Then baste the side seams together. Fig. P

25. With right sides together, sew the pillow top to the pillow back. Finish the seam allowance with a zigzag stitch or a similar stitch.

26. Turn the pillow right side out and sew snap fasteners or hook-and-loop tape closures to the tabs and pillow base.

27. Attach a button to the top of each tab.

28. Insert the pillow form.

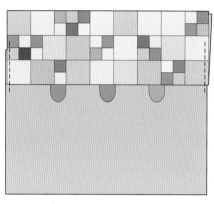

Fig. P

A trio of button tabs enlivens the back of this fanciful pillow.

Now sit back and enjoy a good book!

SQUASH BLOSSOM TABLE RUNNER

Designed and made by Lori Brechlin

I find myself traveling to a simpler place in time—for some reason my heart is firmly planted in this old farmhouse of ours, and in its surrounding fields, woods, and pasture. The inspiration for this project comes from this very place. Every year we grow a small patch of squash and pumpkins and enjoy watching their vines creep along the ground.

MATERIALS

Assorted cotton prints: For background

Dark: 4 pieces 4˝ × 12˝

Medium: 4 pieces 4˝ × 12˝

Light: 3 pieces 4˝ × 12˝

Cotton print: 1 piece 40˝ × 15˝ for backing

Assorted wool scraps: Approximately 8 colors for appliqué—blue, light green, medium green, dark green, white, brown, yellow, and mustard

Cotton thread

Sewing needle

Pins

White copy paper

Instructions

BACKGROUND

Machine or hand stitch the background prints together, using ¼˝ seam allowance, stitching together the long sides. Refer to the project photo (next page) as your guide. Press the seams open and set aside.

WOOL APPLIQUÉ

Use the Squash Blossom Table Runner *patterns (pullout page P1) as instructed.*

1. Make templates by tracing all pattern pieces onto the copy paper. Cut out and trace the templates onto the corresponding wools and cut out on the line.

2. Find the center of the stitched background by folding in half widthwise and finger-press. Center and pin the blue wool heart to the crease of the runner.

Finished table runner: 12″ × 39″

3. Referring to the project photo, pin the wool pieces to the background and stitch in place using cotton thread and a primitive stitch (page 8). Everything doesn't have to match perfectly, so please don't fret if one of the stems is a bit wonkier than the other or if one leaf is lower than the next. You want this to look handmade.

FINISHING

1. Once all the wool pieces are stitched in place, press the front of the appliquéd runner with a hot iron. Now lay the backing fabric facedown on your work surface; lay the runner faceup on top of that, centering the runner top on the backing fabric, and pin in place.

2. Cut the backing fabric to within 1″ all around the edges of the runner top, and fold over twice and stitch the border edge down using a primitive stitch and cotton thread.

3. You may age this project further by dabbing on a little coffee, tea, or walnut stain and letting it dry in the sun.

Quilts

A BIG HOUSE AND A CHERRY TREE

Hand appliquéd and machine pieced and quilted by Renée Plains

Hand appliqué is one of my favorite kinds of stitching to do. This small project has just the right amount of appliqué for a take-along project. The whimsical scale of the chickens and cherries, which are as big as the front door and windows respectively, reminds me of vintage folk art. It's a playful juxtaposition that adds personality to your projects.

MATERIALS
Refer to the quilt assembly diagram (page 65) for the key to the letters.

Appliqué background (A)
Tan plaid: 1 fat quarter

Appliqué pieces
Use the following color scraps:

Dark blue plaid: For house side

Tan plaid: For house front

Red check: For roof

Red stripe: For door

Brown print: For large chicken

Rust print: For small chicken

Red plaid wool: For cherries

Assorted green plaids: For leaves

Tan check: For fence

Assorted blue prints: For birds

Brown print: For tree

Gold plaid: For window openings

Inner top and bottom borders (B)
Blue plaid: ⅛ yard

Inner bottom border (C)
Red plaid: ⅛ yard

Inner side borders (D)
Tan print: ⅛ yard

Inner top border (E)
Rust check: ⅛ yard

Inner bottom border (E)
Brown print: ⅛ yard

Outer pieced borders (F and G)
Assorted brown prints: ¼ yard total

Outer border corner blocks
Red plaid: ⅛ yard

Tan plaid: ⅛ yard

Binding
Brown print: ⅛ yard

Finished quilt: 22″ × 25″

CUTTING

Refer to the quilt assembly diagram (next page) for the key to the letters.

Appliqué background

• Cut 1 rectangle 10½″ × 15″ from tan plaid (A).

Inner borders

• Cut 2 strips 2½″ × 15″ from blue plaid (B).

• Cut 1 strip 2″ × 15″ from red plaid (C).

• Cut 2 strips 2½″ × 16″ from tan print (D).
(For a scrappy look, I randomly pieced one
of the inner borders.)

• Cut 1 strip 2″ × 19″ from brown print (E).

• Cut 1 strip 2″ × 19″ from rust check (E).

Outer side borders

• Cut 2 strips 2″ × 19″ from dark print (F).
(For a scrappy look, I randomly pieced
the borders.)

Outer top and bottom borders

• Cut 2 strips 3½″ × 16″ from dark print (G).
(For a scrappy look, I randomly pieced
the borders.)

Corner blocks in outer border

• Cut 1 strip 2⅜″ × 22″ from tan plaid.

Subcut into 8 squares 2⅜″ × 2⅜″. Then subcut the
squares in half diagonally from corner to corner.

• Cut 1 strip 2⅜″ × 22″ from red plaid.

Subcut into 8 squares 2⅜″ × 2⅜″. Then subcut the
squares in half diagonally from corner to corner.

NOTE *If these are paired and
then cut with the right sides together,
they will be in the correct position
when you're ready to stitch.*

Appliqué pieces

• Cut the *A Big House and a Cherry Tree* appliqué
patterns (pullout page P3) from different color
scraps as instructed.

• Cut 1 rectangle 5½″ × 6½″ from gold plaid for
windows.

Single binding

• Cut 3 strips 1¼″ × width of fabric from brown print.

Sewing

*Refer to the quilt assembly diagram (next page)
for placement.*

1. Sew the 2 (B) strips to the top and bottom of the
tan plaid background (A).

2. Sew the 1 (C) strip to the bottom of the appliqué
background unit.

3. Position the house sections with windows on
the background fabric. Then place a 5½″ × 6½″
gold plaid rectangle behind these sections and
trim any fabric that extends beyond the house.

This piece of fabric creates a warm glow from
inside the house. Using reverse appliqué, sew
the windows. Then appliqué the house to the
background.

4. Appliqué all remaining appliqué pieces to the
tan plaid background (A).

5. Sew 2 (D) strips to the sides of the appliquéd
center.

6. Sew rust check and brown print (E) strips to
the top and bottom of the appliquéd center.

7. Randomly piece 2 (F) strips and cut 2 side 2″ × 19″ outer border strips. Then sew these 2 strips to each side of the appliquéd center.

8. Randomly piece 2 (G) strips and cut 2 top and bottom 3½″ × 16″ outer border strips. Set aside for later.

9. With right sides together, layer a red plaid half-square triangle on top of a tan plaid half-square triangle and sew together. Repeat to make 16 half-square triangle units. Open seams and press. Fig. A

10. Sew 4 half-square triangle units together to make a total of 4 corner border blocks. Fig. B

11. Sew a corner block to each end of a (G) strip (For visual interest, I purposely turned one of the corner blocks in a different position; see the project photo, page 63.) Make 2 border strips.

12. Sew these combined strips to the top and bottom of the quilt center. Fig. C

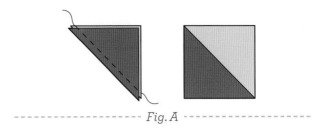

Fig. A

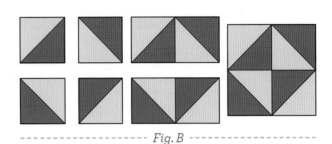

Fig. B

Fig. C

Quilt assembly

Finishing

Sandwich the quilt top, batting, and backing. Quilt as desired. Then bind the quilt.

UP ON THE ROOF

Hand appliquéd and machine quilted by Renée Plains

*Appliquéd much like a penny rug, this wall
quilt is quick to make using pieces of wool. It is
appliquéd with a primitive stitch (page 8), which
resembles a buttonhole stitch (page 8).*

MATERIALS

Appliqué background

Tan check flannel: ¾ yard

Border

Red wool: 1 piece 14˝ × 28˝ (if pieced) or
1 piece 20˝ × 24˝ (if not pieced)

Appliqué pieces

Use the following color scraps:

Red plaid wool: For flower

Gold plaid wool: For flower

Blue plaid wool: For flowers

Green and green plaid wool: For leaves and stems

Green check wool: For flower base, leaves, and stem

Yellow/gold wool: For stars

Blue check and blue plaid wool: For bird

Brown check wool: For roof

Brown wool: For door

Red and red check wool: For house

Yellow/gold print: For windows

Binding

Red plaid: ⅛ yard

Notion

Button: 4 mm wide for bird's eye

Finished quilt: 20˝ × 24˝

CUTTING

Appliqué background

• Cut 1 rectangle 20½˝ × 24½˝ from tan check flannel.

Appliqué pieces

• Cut the *Up on the Roof* appliqué patterns (pullout page P1) from different color scraps as instructed. Fig. A

Wavy border

• Use the *Up on the Roof* wavy border pattern (pullout page P1) to create the 2 halves of the border.

If you are using a …

20˝ × 24˝ red wool piece:
Place the pattern in the upper left corner of the fabric. Trace around the pattern; then turn the pattern over along the A end and continue marking the upper right side of the border. Turn the pattern along the B end and trace again to make the bottom half of the border. Cut the border along the traced lines.

14˝ × 28˝ red wool piece:
Follow the instructions above, but stagger the placement of the pattern, in order to accurately fit the 2 halves of the border pattern. Cut the borders along the traced lines. Fig. B

Single binding

• Cut 3 strips 1¼˝ × width of fabric from red plaid.

Fig. A

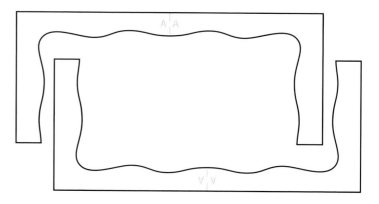

Fig. B

Sewing

1. Referring to the project photo (page 67) for placement, appliqué the pieces to the background fabric using a primitive stitch (page 8). Then attach a button for the bird's eye.

2. Place the 2 border pieces on the appliquéd background and pin in place.

3. Cross-stitch (page 8) over the top and bottom where the 2 border sections meet. (I opted to piece the border so a smaller piece of wool could be used, but you can use a single piece of fabric if you wish.) This makes a nice detail on the border while securely joining the 2 sections.

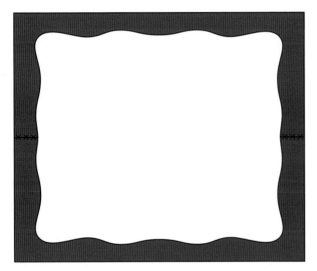

4. Using a primitive stitch, appliqué the inner wavy border edge to the background fabric.

Finishing

Sandwich the quilt top, batting, and backing. Quilt as desired. (I stitched around the appliqué shapes and the wavy edge border with wool thread. For a more primitive look, I used a larger quilting stitch than usual.) Then bind the quilt.

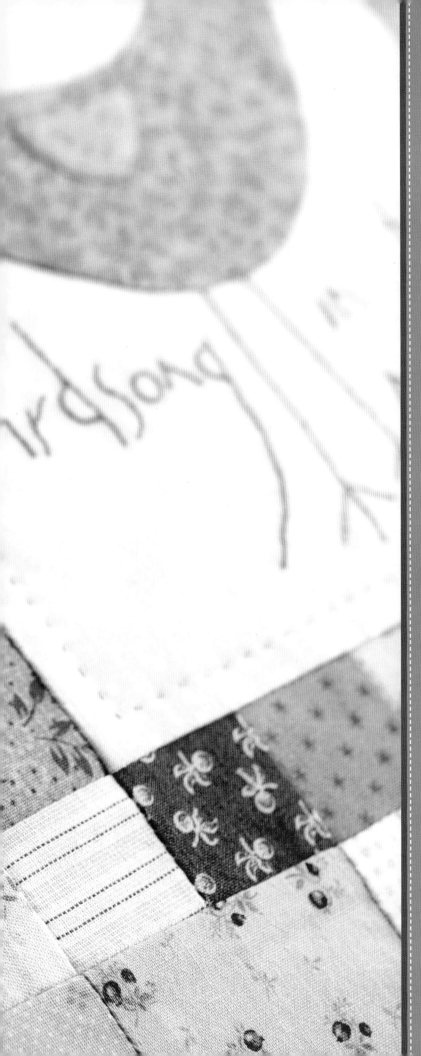

About the Contributors

Lori Brechlin

Cherry Tomato Pinkeep Necklace (page 16) and Squash Blossom Table Runner (page 58) originally appeared in *Summer at Notforgotten Farm* by Lori Brechlin, from Kansas City Star Quilts.

Anni Downs

Embroidered Heart Needle Book (page 30), Flowered Heat Bag (page 36), and Birdsong Pillow (page 52) originally appeared in *Hatched and Patched's Some Kind of Wonderful* by Anni Downs, available from Kansas City Star Quilts.

Debbie Duckworth

Land of the Free Jacket (page 40) originally appeared in *Victory Girls* by Polly Minick and Laurie Simpson, from Kansas City Star Quilts

Betty Edgell

Honey Bee Pincushion (page 18) originally appeared in *Lizzie's Legacy* by Betsy Chutchian, from Kansas City Star Quilts.

Stacy Nash

Slipper and Large Strawberry Pinkeep (page 24) originally appeared in *My Name Is Lidya* by Stacy Nash, from Kansas City Star Quilts.

Renée Plains

Appliqué Basics (page 6), Bird on a Vine Pinkeep (page 12), Little Sparrow Pinkeep (page 20), Out on a Limb Notebook Cover (page 44), Over the Nest Sewing Pocket (page 46), *A Big House and a Cherry Tree* (page 62), and *Up on the Roof* (page 66) originally appeared in *A Bird in Hand* by Renée Plains, from Kansas City Star Quilts.

Marlene Strauser

Wool Pear Pinkeep (page 26) originally appeared in *My Name Is Lidya* by Stacy Nash, from Kansas City Star Quilts.

Want even more creative content?

Make it, snap it, share it
using
#ctpublishing